I'm Divorced Now

Embracing Soul-Nourishing Solitude

4-Year *Anniversary* EDITION

UMM ZAKIYYAH

I'm Divorced Now: Embracing Soul-Nourishing Solitude (4-Year Anniversary Edition)
by Umm Zakiyyah

Order information at **uzuniversity.com** and **uzauthor.com**
UZ Course information at **uzhearthub.com**

Arabic script of Qur'an from legacy.quran.com and corpus.quran.com

Verses from Qur'an adapted from Saheeh International, Darussalam, and Yusuf Ali translations.

Published by Al-Walaa Publications
Dallas, Texas (USA)

TABLE OF CONTENTS

Prologue

A Positive Reframe of Life and Soul

Today, as I write this prologue to this new edition of *I'm Divorced Now*, it has been exactly four years since my Merciful, All-Wise Rabb decreed that I choose the health of my soul over a marriage that was no longer emotionally healthy or spiritually beneficial for me. And it has taken each day of those four years to get to the point where I am today: I have now found peace and tranquility with this blessed challenge that my Merciful Creator has gifted me.

And yes, I now see as a blessed divine gift what my heart previously experienced as a tremendous, soul-crushing loss. As I write this, it's difficult for me to believe that I once could not see beyond my pain, that I once felt like my life was effectively over, and that I once feared I could not go on.

And no, this shift in perspective isn't inspired by any negative epiphanies I've experienced about the soul companion that my Merciful Rabb had gifted me on my sojourn in this world at that time. Rather this shift in perspective is inspired by a series of soul-nourishing epiphanies that I've experienced about the spiritual light every believer is gifted when he or she nurtures *emaan* and *taqwaa* every day of his or her life. In fact, if anything, I find in my heart more compassion and empathy for my former soul companion—and more understanding—because I now have more compassion, empathy, and understanding of myself. Even as I have a deeper appreciation, understanding, and gratitude for the greater good of he and I having our own separate lives and paths today.

So, as I look at this day four years ago, this date on the calendar, I now see it as a day of gratitude, instead of an anniversary of loss, pain, and heartbreak. I now see this date as an anniversary of soul-nourishing goodness. This journey is a spiritually beneficial *khayr* that has taught me so much about life and love, and about what it means to treasure what is most valuable in this world: the health of my soul and the preservation of the sacred relationship I have with my Rabb—the Creator, Owner, and Manager of all that exists.

Readers might recall that the subtitle of the original edition of this book was *Heartbreak and Healing*. However, those words no longer resonate with me personally as I reflect on where I am today, emotionally and spiritually.

No, I do not claim to have absolutely *no* traces of heartbreak within me or to have absolutely *nothing* left to heal. It's just that, at this juncture in my sojourn in this world, the term *soul-nourishing solitude* resonates more deeply in capturing the essence of my current emotional and spiritual relationship with myself than *heartbreak and healing*.

With regards to my healing journey, I believe these words that so many others have expressed on their journey accurately capture where I am on mine: *I have healed enough.*

By the mercy of Allah, I have been blessed to transition from the stage of surviving and healing to the stage of thriving and joyful living. In other words, I am now living daily in a space of soul-nourishing gratitude.

Yes, I still experience moments of emotional pain, especially when something in my external world awakens an emotional memory within my internal world. Yet even in those painful moments, the hurt is fleeting and temporary, and it no longer defines my life and existence. And I am grateful.

So, today I look back at my journey with more gratitude than sadness and with more tranquility than pain. For that reason, the subtitle of this four-year anniversary edition has been upgraded to *Soul-Nourishing Solitude*.

Nevertheless, I would be remiss to deny or trivialize the very real heartbreak and healing that have brought me to this point. For that reason, the core text of the original

edition of this book remains largely intact and unadjusted.
This is my way of paying homage to the hurting and
healing parts of my journey that laid the bricks on the path
of the soul-nourishing solitude that I enjoy today.

Sincerely,
Your sister in faith and love,

Umm Zakiyyah
August 30, 2024
26th of Safar 1446AH

—from the journal of Umm Zakiyyah

Introduction

Sharing My Journey

Though I'm sharing my journey, the truth is, I don't always understand my journey. In fact, most times I don't. So, each day I beg my Merciful Creator to guide my heart as He heals it, and to guide my steps as I take them. I also ask Him for beautiful patience, for I know He is As-Saboor; and I ask Him for sincere gratitude, for I know He is Ash-Shakoor.

Knowing that I have a Merciful, Compassionate, Patient, and All-Wise Rabb is what keeps me going each day. Because the truth is, no matter how "strong" I might appear at times, the repeated trials of life have confused my heart and exhausted my spirit.

Sometimes when I hear the prophetic hadith about there coming a time when a person will walk by a grave and feel jealous of the person inside, I cry. Because I have felt that way so many times.

But I don't think this is a good thing, as we are instructed to not wish for death. And that makes sense, even to my hurting heart, no matter painful my trials sometimes become. Because truly, none of us knows what our fate would be should Allah take our soul at the moment that we are most wishing for an end to all of the emotional suffering.

The reality is, most people will leave this world and just face more pain and suffering than they ever faced during their difficult sojourn on earth. Then they'll find themselves wishing to come back to their earthly home, even if just for a day, to better prepare their soul to meet their Creator. And I don't want that to be me.

In the Qur'an, Allah says:

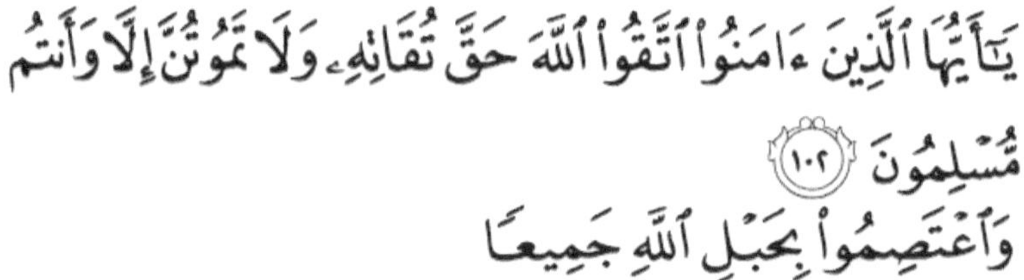

"O you who believe! Fear Allah as He should be feared, and die not except in a state of Islam [as Muslims] with complete submission. And hold fast, all of you together, to the Rope of Allah…"
—*Ali 'Imraan* (3:102-103)

In my own life, I fear that if I do not take this journey of healing, I could allow the repeated emotional wounds upon my heart to distance me from my soul and from fully embracing the merciful gift of *emaan* from my Rabb.

I don't say this to complain. I say this in hopes of you better understanding this journey that I'm sharing with you.

Because it's not easy.

At this stage in my worldly sojourn, I've come to learn that healing in community is so much healthier than healing in silence, isolation, or shame—if only we can find (or create) a healthy healing space for ourselves, as I hope to

do in the UZ Heart & Soul Care community at
uzhearthub.com.

Nevertheless, I know my efforts will be imperfect, and I know that I'll need the guidance and input of others along the way. Yet I am praying that this single effort will support not only myself, but also so many other struggling souls who are on the path of emotional healing and spiritual betterment amidst the painful trials of life.

May Allah be with you on your journey, and may we all meet in Jannah and look back and laugh at what we thought would be our undoing, when Allah only gifted it to us to bring us closer to Him.

Your sister in faith and struggle,
Umm Zakiyyah

PART ONE

Glimpses of Love

"Each time I committed myself to a soul companion in marriage, I committed myself to love—even when the sacred contract did not come to full fruition. So, I uttered 'I love you' to him and meant every word. Now, I'm realizing I should have first uttered those words to myself— and meant every word."

—from the journal of Umm Zakiyyah

<h1 style="text-align:center">1</h1>

<h1 style="text-align:center">In Love with Love</h1>

"How are you doing?" my uncle asked, his expression conveying compassion and concern. I was nineteen years old and sitting across from him in the kitchen of my grandmother's home in Pittsburgh, Pennsylvania, which was home to most of my father's side of the family. I was in my second year of my undergraduate studies at Emory University, and I was visiting my family during the school's winter break.

"I heard you got married, but it didn't work out," he said.

Internally, I cringed at the word "married" being used for the nikaah contract I had done the year before and annulled just months later. Marriage sounded too serious a term for that brief error in judgment. But I didn't correct my uncle. In any case, I wouldn't have known what to tell him to call it instead. My uncle was Christian, so in his world, there was only dating, engagement, or marriage; and I wouldn't call my nikaah contract any of those things. And naturally, nikaah was not a term he was familiar with.

Years later, I would refer to the brief nikaah contract as "that situation that happened when was eighteen years old." Today I sometimes wryly think of it as an unhealthy emotional entanglement because, truly, that's all it was;

but not marriage. Till today, marriage seems too dignified a term for that experience.

"I'm better now," I told my uncle honestly.

"What happened?" he said.

"Looking back," I said, "I realize I wasn't in love. But I was in love with being in love."

His eyebrows rose in understanding, and he nodded reflectively. "It's good that you understand that at such a young age," he said. "It takes a lot of people years to know the difference."

But as I reflect on my "love journey" today, I realize that my heart remains a student of what love truly is, and it has so much more to learn.

"The wise do not consider the chains and shackles of jail to be the toughest restraints. The chains of attachment are the strongest of the ties that bind."

—Thich Nhat Hanh, *Fidelity: How to Create a Loving Relationship That Lasts*

Personal Reflection:
What thoughts do you have about "being in love with love"? Can you relate? Why or why not?

2

The Signs Aren't Always Hidden

Before embarking on my journey of emotional healing, I was blessed with one soul companion in marriage, and I was tested with one "almost marriage" at eighteen years old. Today I view that "almost marriage" as more an error in judgment than a healthy relationship choice. However, I continue to draw benefit from it today.

Though short-lived, that cancelled *nikaah* contract taught me so much about what I don't want in a soul companion in marriage. But most importantly, it taught me about what I don't want in a relationship with myself.

In the few short months that the *nikaah* contract lasted, I became a shell of myself. In that relationship, I was tested with the most toxic relationship with a man that I would ever have in life.

During that time, this man (whom I'll call Jabbar) personified in so many ways what mental health professionals would call "narcissism" today. But I didn't know any of those fancy terms back then. I just knew (or at least I would come to learn) that Jabbar saw the world through only his eyes and was convinced that it was my religious duty to fit into that narrow vision.

I first met Jabbar at a Muslim retreat that I was invited to during my first year in college when I was seventeen years old. A couple of days into the retreat, Jabbar approached me saying that he was interested in talking to me for marriage. What I didn't know at the time was that earlier that day, Jabbar had been present when a friend of his (whom I'll call Adam) spoke to my elder brother (who was also at the retreat) seeking permission to speak to me for marriage. But by the time I learned this, I'd already agreed to speak to Jabbar.

When my elder brother found out what happened, he was furious. "What Jabbar did was wrong," he said. "He knew his friend had already asked about you. Then he went behind my back and spoke to you without saying a word to me or his friend."

"I didn't know that," I told him honestly.

"But you should've asked me first," he said. "I was right next door in the brothers' villa."

I furrowed my brows in distaste. "*Ask* you?" I said. "Why would I need to ask you before I talk to someone?"

"That's how things are done in Islam. A woman isn't supposed to speak to a man for marriage unless her father gives his permission," he said. "And since Dad isn't here right now, that responsibility falls on me."

Hearing this took me aback. To my ignorant teenage ears at the time, everything my brother was saying sounded so archaic and "cultural."

In the predominantly African-American Muslim community that we were part of at the time, we prided ourselves in not following the "cultural Islam" of so Muslim immigrants from the Arab and Desi world.

When our parents accepted Islam after they got married and transitioned from the Nation of Islam to orthodox Islam (like thousands of other Black American Muslims), they'd committed themselves and our family to practicing Islam in a way that preserved their American identity and our modern cultural reality. Yet to me, everything my brother was saying sounded like something straight out of an Arab or Indian history book. Had he lost his mind? I thought.

"You should stop talking to Jabbar and talk to Adam instead."

"Why?" I asked rhetorically, offended at the suggestion.

"Because Adam did things the right way, and Jabbar didn't."

Hearing what my brother was saying did give me pause, as I agreed that what Jabbar did was incorrect. But I didn't see how Jabbar's error in judgment made it an obligation for me to speak to Adam instead. I wasn't attracted to Adam, so I had no desire to speak to him, no matter how honorable his approach and intentions.

"But isn't it my choice who I talk to?" I said.

"Not really," my brother said. "At least if we're going by the Sunnah. But of course, you can't be forced into any marriage, so that part is your choice. But you shouldn't be talking to Jabbar in the first place, so he shouldn't even be given a chance."

It would be years before I could appreciate the deep Islamic wisdom in my elder brother's perspective. But at seventeen years old, all I could hear was my brother saying he wanted to control my life and tell me who I could and could not talk to, and I wasn't about to listen to that.

"It's so difficult, isn't it? To see what's going on when you're in the absolute middle of something? It's only with hindsight we can see things for what they are."
—S.J. Watson, *Before I Go to Sleep*

Personal Reflection:
Have you ever missed obvious warning signs before making a significant life decision? Looking back, what do you think made you miss the signs? What have you learned from the experience that benefits you today?

3

Mistakes and Wrong Choices

After the Muslim retreat ended, I returned to my college campus dormitory, and Jabbar returned to the apartment near his own college that he shared with Adam and one other friend. Despite my brother repeatedly expressing his deep disappointment and disagreement with my decision, I continued communicating with Jabbar and considered the possibility of marrying him.

By then, I'd spoken to my father about what my elder brother was saying. In the conversations I had with my father, it was clear that he was trying to be diplomatic amidst my teenage hotheadedness. On the one hand, he understood my brother's point of view (and agreed with it though he didn't admit it aloud). On the other hand, he understood my own point of view due to how he and my mother had raised me and my sisters to think for ourselves and make our own decisions in life, especially for something as serious as marriage.

I recall my father expressing some concerns but ultimately giving his blessings. But even at seventeen years old, I could tell that my father disapproved of Jabbar. However, due to my father's foresightedness, wisdom, and life experience, he was more afraid of losing me to the world than to a bad marriage choice. So, he decided to support me in protecting my soul instead of opposing my wishes and thus risking pushing me to compromise it.

At that time, it was the early 1990's, and the situation amongst the Muslims in the United States was similar to how it is today. Many of the Muslim youth who were my peers had rebelled against their parents' Muslim lifestyle and had chosen a life of "sexual freedom" instead.

Growing up, my father and mother had always expressed the point of view—to their daughters *and* sons—that marrying young is much better than falling into the sin of fornication, ever. My father repeatedly emphasized that sexual sin affected your soul in ways you couldn't even fathom at the time you're falling into it, so he consistently cautioned us against it.

"Don't choose a lifetime of consequences for a moment of pleasure," my father would say. And I'd listen with my heart and thus was determined to preserve my chastity and reserve sexual intimacy for only a soul companion in marriage. I just wish I'd had more wisdom in choosing who that husband should be.

"Everybody makes mistakes," I reflected one day to my sister years later as we both spoke regretfully about some of the bad decisions we'd made in our life.

"That's true," she said tentatively. "But I'm beginning to learn that there's a difference between mistakes and wrong choices."

I listened, curious as to what she meant.

"A mistake is when you do something wrong and you didn't know any better," she said. "But a wrong choice is when you know full well what is right, but you choose what is wrong instead."

I considered the profound veracity in her words. "That's true," I said thoughtfully, recalling some of my own wrong choices in life.

"And the truth is," she added, "so much of what we call 'mistakes' are really just wrong choices."

"There's no need to regret mistakes you made as a result of being a human being and trying your level best, and failing. Regret only when you are too proud, lazy, or sinful to learn from them."

—from the journal of Umm Zakiyyah

Personal Reflection:
Is there a mistake that you made in the past that still makes you feel ashamed of yourself today? How do you work through the feelings of shame to extract the bigger lesson?

4

Losing Myself to the Mirage of Marriage

In retrospect, I can see that I didn't like Jabbar all that much, but I enjoyed the attention. At seventeen years old, I had no idea what it meant to genuinely connect with another soul in a meaningful way. So, I was more in love with the idea of being in love than I was with Jabbar as a person, as I would tell my Christian uncle later. But hindsight is 20-20. It's the present that blurs the reality of what is right in front of you.

Jabbar was only eighteen years old at the time himself, so he wasn't any more experienced than I was in the subject of love. But he presented himself like he understood so much more than I did about everything, and in my naiveté, I listened to his point of view like it was the absolute truth.

Other than Jabbar's utter disregard for Islamic etiquette and brotherhood when approaching me for marriage, one of the first warning signs of the toxic relationship that I was about to walk into came during a conversation on the phone with Jabbar. I recall relaxing in my dormitory that evening, feeling flattered that Jabbar had called me. But then during the course of the conversation, he said something about wanting an "obedient wife."

There was something in the way that he said this that made my stomach churn. But I didn't fully grasp what was disturbing me, so I explained as best as could. "I don't like the word obedient," I told him.

"Well, that's the word Allah uses," he said in an accusatory term, as if challenging me to go against my Creator.

I immediately backed down and shrank inside, feeling so ashamed of myself. Internally, I sought forgiveness for my blunder and was determined to never take issue with the word "obedient" again. In fact, I made a silent promise to Allah that I would strive my best to be an "obedient wife" since that's what He required of me.

Weeks later, Jabbar called and asked if I'd want my family and friends at our wedding if we got married. I immediately said, "Yes," imagining the ideal wedding ceremony I'd somehow pictured since childhood.

Jabbar's voice became noticeably upset, and he began to scold me. "Why do you need your family and friends there?" he said, speaking as if I'd suggested having an archenemy of his perform the ceremony itself. "I should be the only one who matters to you if we're getting married," he said sternly. "I'll be your husband."

Taken aback, I stammered a meek apology. But when I hung up, I knew with certainty that I still wanted my family and friends there. I didn't see the point in getting married if I couldn't have the people I loved most involved.

But day after day, Jabbar wore me down with guilt trips and insults until I reluctantly agreed to marry him with no family or friends there, feeling that this perhaps was what it meant to walk the path of an "obedient wife."

"Our most painful relationships, we have learned, have assisted us on the journey to healing, even if they did little more than point out our own issues or show us what we don't want in life."

—Melody Beattie, *The Language of Letting Go*

Personal Reflection:
Have you ever been pressured into doing something that you really didn't want to do? Looking back, what do you think made you cave in? How are you learning to speak up for yourself better today?

5

Forever Girl

When I got married at twenty years old to a close family friend I'd known since childhood, I expected to be married forever. I'd already gone through that painful, albeit short-lived, "almost marriage" to Jabbar when I was eighteen years old, and I wanted this time to be different.

My parents never divorced each other, so I didn't expect to ever be divorced myself. As I mentioned earlier, I didn't think of the brief *nikaah* contract I'd done at eighteen years old to be a real marriage. So I didn't think of myself as "divorced" (at least not in the full sense of the term) by the time I married my childhood friend (whom I'll call Abdullah).

Till today, I think of my marriage to Abdullah as my first marriage, and it was a marriage I imagined would stand the test of time.

All the ingredients were right: Both families encouraged and wanted to the marriage (even before he and I did). Abdullah and I came from similar family backgrounds, had the same ethnicity and culture, and we shared a common spiritual and social outlook on life. And it didn't hurt that we were attracted to each other.

Though I often refer to Abdullah as a "childhood friend," the truth is, he and I weren't particularly close growing up. Abdullah and I were friends in the loose, family-friend meaning of the term. We never spent any time alone together, and any time we spoke to each other, it was with dozens of family members around us. And we almost never spoke to each other. It was our parents who shared a closer, more meaningful bond.

So, I didn't know Abdullah all too well, and he didn't know me all too well either. But our parents and families knew each other well, and I found comfort and reassurance in that.

Being the planner that I was, I embarked on my marriage to Abdullah imagining that I could do everything necessary to ensure that our marriage lasted, *bi'idhnillah*. So I thought of all the reasons that most marriages didn't last, and I was determined to avoid each and every one of those pitfalls.

At the time, I was still young and naïve enough to believe that having a lasting marriage was as simple as marrying a "good man" and being determined to stand by his side, no matter what.

After Abdullah and I got married, I thought to myself: *Now that I have a good husband, I'm determined to be a good wife.*

At the time, to me, being a good wife meant being a giving, generous woman who day after day threw herself into humble self-sacrifice for the sake of "happily ever after." A "good wife" also served and obeyed her husband, and she always put her needs and desires aside to make sure her husband was happy and content.

For years, I'd heard the saying, "Behind every successful man is a good woman," and I was determined to be *that* woman.

So I entered my relationship with Abdullah in the spirit of exhaustive self-sacrifice, imagining that this was the foolproof plan for a marriage that would last forever. During most of our seventeen-year marriage, I naively imagined that through my exhaustive sacrifice and continuous servitude, I would be his "forever girl."

But years later, I would learn that, in reality, exhaustive self-sacrifice is just the foolproof plan to lasting emotional distress—and this distress often outlives the marriage itself.

"In recovery, we learn that self-care leads us on the path to God's will and plan for our life. Self-care never leads away from our higher good; it leads toward it."

—Melody Beattie, *The Language of Letting Go*

Personal Reflection:
What thoughts do you have about "exhaustive self-sacrifice"? Have you ever experienced this in a relationship, or with family or friends? How did you recognize it? Do you feel that you can now better embrace self-care instead?

PART TWO

Heartbreak

"O Allah, I beg You to heal my heart, for You are the One who heals, leaving no traces of brokenness. O Allah, I beg You to purify my heart, for You are the One who purifies, leaving no traces of impurity…"

—from the journal of Umm Zakiyyah

6

Hidden Patterns Threaded in Pain

My brief *nikaah* contract with Jabbar remains one of the most embarrassing, humiliating memories of my youth. There are still moments till today that I can hardly believe I allowed myself to be manipulated by him time and time again.

When I think of that dark time in my life, I sometimes refer to it as "hitting my head." That's how much sense that "almost marriage" makes to me even now.

But as I continue my healing journey today after parting from my second soul companion, I'm beginning to understand that my brief relationship with Jabbar wasn't as off-kilter as I'd initially imagined.

Like so many African-Americans who grew up in the 1970's and 80's, I came from a "tough love" home, where blind obedience to elder authority was considered basic respect.

In this tough love culture, my deepest emotional feelings and needs were rarely (if ever) acknowledged, let alone nourished. In fact, any sign of them was often punishable if they happened to offend my elders, especially my father.

"We had an intellectual and spiritual upbringing," I told my former soul companion one day, "not an emotional or compassionate one."

In my childhood home, my job as a daughter was pretty much to just "keep quiet and do as you're told." So, most of my interactions with my parents were one-way transactions: me fulfilling their demands. And most of my verbal interactions consisted of two words to either parent: "Yes, sir" or "No, sir" and "Yes, ma'am" or "No, ma'am." The rare exceptions to this occurred during discussions that centered around topics that quite obviously placed my father as the ultimate lawgiver and decision maker in my life, like the ones I had with him about Jabbar.

I don't say this to cast blame on my parents. Today I understand that healing emotional wounds isn't about placing blame. It's about recognizing the sources of pain and acknowledging how their threads are entangled throughout our lived experience, especially as adults seeking love and companionship.

Years ago, I wrote this reflection in my journal: *Being honest with yourself about the source of your pain and blaming someone for your pain are two entirely different things.*

When there is transgenerational trauma—as all descendants of slavery and survivors of generational oppression and racism have suffered (coined PTSS, post-traumatic slave syndrome by Dr. Joy DeGruy)—then there must be transgenerational healing. Thus, the stages of healing that we normally associate with the stages of one person's life will often manifest throughout the stages of each generation.

In my understanding, these stages can manifest as follows: Stage one is living in trauma. Stage two is living in survival mode in response to that trauma. Stage three is seeking healing as a way to free oneself from survival mode. And stage four is thriving beyond the unhealthy states of trauma and survival.

Looking back on my own life, I believe my parents and their parents lived simultaneously in stages one and two (trauma and survival mode), and "tough love" was their generation's most logical and effective survival-mode response to transgenerational (and ongoing) trauma.

Growing up, tough love meant that children were expected to obey their parents and elders while suppressing (or dismissing) their own emotional feelings and personal needs. This was for the "higher good" of serving, honoring, and pleasing those whom God placed in authority over them.

Moreover, any home that imbibed this tough love—with children willingly sacrificing themselves and repressing their emotions for the sake of their parents—was considered the hallmark of a "good family." Consequently, this type of childrearing was implemented by the most upstanding, self-respecting African-Americans during that time, especially those deeply involved in the church, as my parents' childhood homes were.

My father was born in 1937, and my mother was born in 1946. This was a time in United States history that was one of the most tumultuous and dangerous (literally) for Black Americans, especially upstanding, successful and self-respecting ones like my parents and their families. So, the mindset that my parents were raised on was one of surviving the brutality of White racism while becoming as successful as possible in an environment that was rigged against you.

Naturally, for my parents and their parents, their top priority was to keep their children alive and safe, not to delve into existential questions about their children's outlook on life, or about their children's emotional health and elusive "feelings." Their children's very survival and safety depended on blind obedience to Black authority, irrespective of how you *felt* about what you were being told, or about the choices those in authority were making.

For this reason, it is only natural that my parents raised me and my siblings upon this type of tough love, which (prayerfully) ensured our survival and safety, as well as gave us the greatest opportunity for worldly success in a White-dominated society.

Unfortunately, however, this type of childrearing had the unintended side effect of making me feel that I didn't have a right to honor my own deepest desires and needs, particularly if they conflicted with the demands or desires of anyone with a divinely mandated role of superiority over me. Given that my faith tradition taught that men are the leaders of the home and society, I felt it was my religious duty to show deference to them, even if this resulted in my own internal suffering.

So, I entered each marriage (and "almost marriage") with the mindset of exhaustive self-sacrifice while disappearing so much of my deepest self from existence—even when my husband didn't explicitly ask this from me. But he didn't have to. I'd been raised to assume that my emotional disappearance was an essential part of fulfilling my duty to the one taking care of me—even when he wasn't actually taking care of me in the manner that our Creator mandated.

And, truth be told, each of my husbands loved and cherished this about me, even when he ostensibly supported my own personal aspirations. In fact, the very breakdown of each soul companionship and marriage contract occurred when having my own needs met would require a level of sacrifice from my husband that he was either unable or unwilling to give.

Personal Reflection:
What part of your childhood do you believe has shown up in unhealthy ways in your adult relationships? How did you come to recognize it? How are you healing today?

7
Lost and Confused

When Abdullah and I broached our seventeenth year of marriage, I asked for a *khula'* (female initiated marriage dissolution). I was emotionally spent, mentally exhausted, and spiritually hanging on by a thread. I also felt—like so many women who give up too much of themselves—that I wasn't fully appreciated.

In retrospect, in all fairness, I can't say with any certainty that this perception was correct. At the time, I didn't know anything about love languages and what they meant for me and Abdullah personally. Most importantly, I didn't know much about myself.

But looking back, I can say with relative certainty that I didn't fully love and appreciate myself during all those years of exhaustive self-sacrifice.

And I know now that you can't experience true, soul-nourishing love and appreciation until you first love and appreciate yourself.

Yet till today, even with all I've learned about myself and true love, I continue to believe that Abdullah and I were never meant to last forever, though I'd initially imagined otherwise. He was a temporary comfort and test for me, as I was for him.

But when I first felt the weight of knowing that Abdullah and I had to go our separate ways, I felt so lost and confused, and abandoned and alone. And so many parts of me felt angry and disappointed in him. In my mind, there was so much *he* could have done differently and so much that *he* should have done differently. But today, I see that the biggest change that needed to happen at that time in my life was a transformation within myself. He was walking his imperfect path, as I was walking mine; so there was no need to cast blame.

It took years of healing before my heart found peace with this advice to my own struggling soul that I wrote in my personal journal:

> *Don't fault a temporary comfort for being temporary. They couldn't have been anything else. Whether it's death, illness, unforeseen circumstances, or human choice, your loved ones are leaving you whether you like it or not. Not even they can control what is written for them. So focus on what is written for you. Yes, you can cry and vent, or feel sad and disappointed. But don't blame them for not being God. Because only your Creator has the ability to* always *be there for you.*

Today I also reflect often on this beautiful prophetic hadith that is a consistent reminder to my struggling, restless soul: Sahl ibn Sa'ad reported that the Angel Gabriel came to the Prophet, *sallallaahu 'alaihi wa sallam,* and said:

"O Muhammad, live as you wish, for you will die. Work as you wish, for you will be repaid accordingly. Love whomever you wish, for you will be separated. Know that the nobility of the believer is in prayer at night and his honor is in his independence of people" (al-Mu'jam al-Aswaat 4410, hasan by Al-Albaani).

"Recognize when a phase, job, a life stage, or a relationship is over and let it go. Allow yourself to gracefully exit situations you have outgrown. Moving on doesn't have to be a catastrophic, dramatic event. You can simply choose to move forward with peace and clarity."

—Quote via @thebehappyproject (Instagram)

Personal Reflection:
What thoughts do you have about letting go and moving on with peace and clarity? Have you ever had to make this difficult choice? What did you learn from it?

<h1 style="text-align:center">8</h1>

What Are You Investing In?

During the seventeen years that I was married to Abdullah, it wasn't only my marriage that I approached with exhaustive self-sacrifice. It was how I approached nearly all of my relationships.

Whether it was in my teaching, my friendships, my family, or my faith community, I felt that my goodness and piety rested in putting others' needs and desires before my own. And over time, I paid for it mightily—emotionally, mentally, and spiritually.

Today, when I look back at my mindset of continuous self-sacrifice in servitude to my husband and others— whom I deemed more important than myself—I want to ask that naïve, giving heart of mine, "What are you investing in, exactly?"

I don't mean this sarcastically. I mean it in the spirit of self-honesty and emotional healing today. I don't want to continue to exhaust myself in self-sacrifice—literally—such that I have little to no "self" left after the sacrifice.

Sacrificing something sincerely for the sake of Allah is one thing, but sacrificing your very *self* to please another person—or to have a lasting marriage, to secure a friendship, or to please a religious group or teacher—is another entirely. Healthy sacrifice nourishes the soul and rejuvenates the heart, while toxic sacrifice wounds the soul and exhausts the heart.

When I embarked on my healing journey many years ago, I wrote these two reflections in my journal:

Suffering is not the same as sacrifice. Know yourself. Know your limits. Draw the line.

• • •

You cannot give of a self that does not exist. Thus, self-care and self-preservation must be essential to your life if you wish to truly give of yourself to others. You cannot give charity from wealth that does not encompass your possessions, and you cannot give from a spirit that does not encompass your being. So invest in your emotional, physical, and spiritual wealth.
You can only spend from what you have.

And today, I'm committed to investing in my own emotional and spiritual health so that I can spend more healthily and freely from an ever-expanding emotional and spiritual wealth resource, *bi'idhnillaah.*

When I take care of the deepest needs of my own heart and soul first and foremost, as my Merciful Rabb has instructed each of us to do, then I am better able to generously give to others without exhausting my deepest needs and life sources in the least. This is because, ultimately, self-care isn't about relying on your own limited resources in exhaustive self-sacrifice; it's about humbly, vulnerably and consistently seeking help and strength from God's unlimited resources before offering anything of your own to His creation.

This is the first step to true self-love and self-care, as well as to healthy sacrifice and blessed generosity, and it requires the establishment of healthy boundaries—with others and within yourself.

"Boundaries are vital to recovery. Having and setting healthy limits is connected to all phases of recovery: growing in self-esteem, dealing with feelings, and learning to really love and value ourselves."

—Melody Beattie, *The Language of Letting Go*

Personal Reflection:
Have you ever had to establish boundaries in a close relationship after having been a continuous "giver" for so long? Did you find the transition difficult or emotionally painful? Why or why not?

9

A Miracle in My Life

After my marriage to Abdullah came to an end, I found myself facing multiple trials that I never imagined I would: I was a divorced single mother, I was falling deeper and deeper into depression, and I was doubting my faith and ability to be Muslim.

During the latter part of my marriage to Abdullah, he and I had lived as American expats in Riyadh, Saudi Arabia, along with our daughter. So, once the marriage crumbled, our then teenage daughter and I returned to the United States alone. At the time, I had no home of my own because my husband and I had left everything to "make *hijrah* to a Muslim land" and thus had no plans on ever returning.

But Allah had other plans, at least for me.

When my daughter and I first arrived back in Maryland, we stayed briefly with my husband's mother, but this was naturally going to be short-lived (at least on my part). As Abdullah and I finalized the divorce, my daughter stayed with her grandmother, and I moved in with a friend who allowed me to sleep on her couch until I could find a home of my own. I eventually found residence in the basement of a Muslim women's homeless shelter, where I volunteered my time to support the other women living there.

During this time, I worked with the manager of the shelter, who would later become my second soul companion in marriage, a bond that would last six years total. At the time that he and I married, I was barely holding on to my *emaan*, and I felt that my very existence was a burden to my loved ones, to the Muslim community, and to the world itself. It was during this time that I nearly took my own life.

But Allah had other plans and sent divine intervention in the form of a man—my second soul companion (whom I'll call Karam). Later, I would often refer to Karam as my Miracle due to how Allah used his presence to nurse me back to emotional and spiritual life.

I think the first time that I actually really saw Karam for the tremendous blessing he would later be to my life was when we were working together at the shelter one day, and he said to me will full conviction and sincerity, "I would die protecting you."

His words touched a deep part of me, and my eyes widened in surprise. "Who are you, and where did you come from?" I asked him in all honesty, with not a trace of sarcasm in my voice.

He then explained that he saw me as a gift to the ummah and that it was his duty, as well as the duty of all

Muslim men, to make sure that a woman like me was cared for and protected so that I could continue to share my voice with the world.

Before this moment, I felt virtually invisible to men, except as an object of sexual *fitnah*, as a social or religious commodity to advance their own agendas, or as a potential "wife servant" in marriage. Before meeting Karam, I had been consistently rejected and emotionally abandoned by so many of those I'd imagined would love and protect me. So, meeting Karam really was like a real-life miracle, and I was convinced that he was my soul mate.

"There are memories that time does not erase... Forever does not make loss forgettable, only bearable."
—Cassandra Clare, *City of Heavenly Fire*

Personal Reflection:
What are your thoughts on the concept of a "soul mate"? Do you think it is real? If so, do you believe a person can have more than one soul mate in life? Why or why not?

10

The Final Break

During our time together, I felt a level of love and connection with Karam that I never had in my life. He fulfilled so many of my needs that I had given up on in this transient world.

But even this miraculous connection had cracks, and we ultimately divorced after about five years of marriage, only to come back together and remarry after being divorced for about a year.

It was during that one year that Karam and I were divorced before remarrying that I entered into an "almost marriage" contract in a long-distance relationship that I would dissolve shortly after it had begun.

In the end, I imagine that neither Karam nor I ever recovered fully from that first break and all the external and internal factors that had pulled us apart.

Today, I now see that I entered every single soul companionship and "almost marriage" in a state of unhealed emotional trauma while seeking a male hero in my life. Somewhere in my subconscious, I imagined that this "male hero" would make up for all the emotional abandonment I'd felt since childhood and that he would always be there for me, no matter what.

Of course, I was wrong.

The truth is, there are no human heroes coming to save you in this world—except your own self saving your own self, with the help of Allah. So, any love story that begins with the assumption that someone else is going to love you more than you love yourself (even if this lack of self-love is subconscious) is bound to end in heartbreak—and quite likely, a very painful divorce.

Karam and I were no different.

In a severe emotional trial of this nature, it is only those men and women who *both* turn the lens inward and own up to their individual manifestations of unhealed childhood trauma—whether as a hero needing to save someone, or as a victim needing a hero to save them—who can have true reconciliation and save their marriages while also saving (and healing) themselves.

This is what I think on when I reflect on the *ayah* in the Qur'an where Allah says:

وَإِنْ خِفْتُمْ شِقَاقَ بَيْنِهِمَا فَٱبْعَثُوا۟ حَكَمًا مِّنْ أَهْلِهِۦ وَحَكَمًا مِّنْ أَهْلِهَآ إِن يُرِيدَآ إِصْلَٰحًا يُوَفِّقِ ٱللَّهُ بَيْنَهُمَآ إِنَّ ٱللَّهَ كَانَ عَلِيمًا خَبِيرًا ﴿٣٥﴾

"And if you fear dissension between the two, send an arbitrator from his people and an arbitrator from her people. If they both desire reconciliation, Allah will cause it between them. Indeed, Allah is ever Knowing and Acquainted [with all things]."
—*An-Nisaa'* (4:35)

In reflecting on the deep wisdom in this *ayah*, I've come to realize that desiring reconciliation is completely different from merely not wanting to get a divorce. Reconciliation requires work and sacrifice, and most of that work is internal.

However, when a marriage reaches a breaking point (which nearly all marriages do), it's easy for any of us, whether male or female, to sit back and say, "I wasn't the one who asked for a divorce!" or "But you did such and such!"

But what's tremendously difficult is to look deep within and admit the part you played in pushing that other person to even feel the need to get a divorce. It's also tremendously difficult to be honest about the very damaging things you yourself did to cause the marriage to break—even if you're the one seeking the divorce.

Furthermore, it's also tremendously difficult to sit back, step outside of your pride and hurt feelings, and commit to true sacrifice.

This is a life-altering, soul nourishing sacrifice that you commit to for the sake of your own emotional health, for the emotional health of your spouse, and for the long-term health and endurance of your marriage. However, so many of us are unable to do this because we are so much more viscerally aware of the *other* person's faults and wrongdoing than we are of our own. And then there's the issue of "I want what I want, no matter who's going to get hurt and no matter what it will cost this marriage."

This is something that men in particular need to pay attention to, especially when they are fixating on polygyny as their perpetual right instead of focusing on their role of *qawwaam* to their current wife (or wives) as their divinely mandated responsibility—something which they will stand before Allah for and answer for on the Day of Judgment.

In describing the perpetual desires and selfish demands of both men and women—which so many of us expect our spouses to just sit by and sacrifice their own emotional and spiritual health for—Allah says:

وَأُحْضِرَتِ ٱلْأَنفُسُ ٱلشُّحَّ

"...And human souls are swayed by greed"
—*An-Nisaa'* (4:128)

"I guess that's just part of loving people: You have to give things up. Sometimes you even have to give them up."
—Lauren Oliver, *Delirium*

Personal Reflection:
When you think of healthy sacrifice in the soul companionship of marriage, what comes to mind? In what

ways would this sacrifice manifest differently for men and women?

PART THREE

Loving and Letting Go

"There are so many ways to be brave in this world. Sometimes bravery involves laying down your life for something bigger than yourself, or for someone else. Sometimes it involves giving up everything you have ever known, or everyone you have ever loved, for the sake of something greater. But sometimes it doesn't.
Sometimes it is nothing more than gritting your teeth through pain, and the work of every day, the slow walk toward a better life. That is the sort of bravery I must have now."

—Veronica Roth, *Allegiant*

11

Gathering the Strength to Leave

"How did you find the strength to leave?" so many people ask when I speak about my divorce. But in my personal journey in life, I've found the concept of "strength" to be more mirage and myth than any tangible goal or reality I could grasp onto.

For this reason, till today, when I know I need to do something challenging or painful, I don't draw on strength so much as I draw on faith. And I consistently find faith to be so much more dependable and effective than any strength I could muster within myself.

Even weak faith is exponentially more powerful than any amount of human strength.

In this, it's like those popular sayings that go something like, "Do it scared. Do it weak. Do it unprepared. But just do it."

A few years ago, a friend of mine contacted me about a toxic relationship with a potential husband whom she felt addicted to. She knew she had to let him go, but she felt too weak to. As we spoke, she told me, "I don't think I'm strong enough to cut him off." So I told her, "You don't need to be strong enough to cut him off. You just need to cut him off. Then you can cry yourself to sleep every night whenever you feel weak."

In those moments in life when I myself tried to be "strong enough" before I did what I knew I needed to do, I've found that waiting for strength was more a roadblock than a pathway to any genuine success. Worse still, waiting for strength gave my struggling soul yet another excuse to abandon myself emotionally and spiritually, as I could always say in all honesty and humility, "I'm not strong enough yet."

Nevertheless, I do continuously pray for strength. I just don't wait for it. Because sometimes strength comes *after* the first step, not before it. Sometimes it even comes after the thousandth step. And sometimes it never comes—at least not in the form we expect.

In any case, who is ever really "strong enough" to do anything difficult or painful? Any real challenge in life will always call for more faith than strength. Even prophets and other righteous people in history were more faithful than "strong." We can see this clearly in the story of Prophet Moses (peace be upon him) when he felt fear in his heart when he knew he had to stand before the tyrannical Pharaoh. It was not personal strength that carried him through, but strong faith.

Though I certainly don't think of my faith as strong, it was also my own faith (however weak) that carried me through this last divorce, and continues to till today.

In reflecting on that difficult moment of finally leaving Karam—a person I called my Miracle and soul mate and whom I loved more deeply than I could comprehend— I wrote this note in my personal journal:

I didn't gather the strength to leave. I lost the strength to stay. My body, mind, and spirit were suffering so much wounding that their very life depended on leaving. They were too broken and weak to withstand any more harm, even if from a soul that meant well.

"It's not hard to decide what you want your life to be about. What's hard, she said, is figuring out what you're willing to give up in order to do the things you really care about."
— Shauna Niequist, *Bittersweet*

Personal Reflection:
Has your emotional or physical health ever suffered as you tried to hold on to someone or something that was clearly no longer healthy for you? Did you finally let go and choose yourself? If so, how are you loving yourself today?

12

What About My Needs and Desires?

When I think on all the exhaustive self-sacrifice I offered upon entering each soul companionship of marriage (and "almost marriage"), I ask my naïve, giving heart, "What are you investing in, exactly?"

In this, I'm really asking my past self: *Which part of this sacrifice is nourishing your own deepest needs and desires? Which part of this sacrifice is investing in your own betterment and future self? What are you getting out of this, truly?*

In our faith communities, we often brush aside these sorts of questions, saying, "We should do everything for the sake of Allah, not for personal or worldly gain." But the truth is, there are some parts of our personal and spiritual life that we should in fact do for personal or worldly gain, and this intention is part of doing that deed for the sake of Allah.

If we take an honest look at our most intimate investments in the soul companionship of marriage, we will see that this worldly-spiritual overlap in benefit and reward is not only present, but at the heart of much of the relationship.

For example, if a man buys a gift for his wife, he wants the worldly gain of making his wife happy and perhaps even the personal gain of spending intimate quality time with her. In this, his good deed clearly has a direct worldly and personal benefit. However, when the man does this from a place of genuine love and compassion for his wife, this act in itself is pleasing to Allah and can thus earn the husband many blessings.

Similarly, if a man wishes to enjoy sexual intimacy with his wife, there is nothing wrong with this. In fact, we know from the prophetic Sunnah that *halaal* intimacy is a means of not only fulfilling one's personal desires, but also of earning blessings in front of our Merciful Creator.

In a famous hadith, Prophet Muhammad (peace and blessings be upon him) said, "…Having intercourse [with one's wife] is *sadaqah.*" They (the Companions) said, "O Messenger of Allah, if one of us fulfills his desire, is there reward in that?" He said, "Do you not see that if he does it in a *haraam* way he will have the burden of sin? So if he does it in a *halaal* way, he will have a reward for that" (Muslim, 1674).

The challenge is, so many of us were taught (directly or indirectly) that when it comes to the needs and desires of women, females shouldn't be seeking things to make themselves happy or to fulfill their desires, even if it's the pleasurable release of sexual intimacy with her husband.

We are taught that as women, our blessings come from making the man happy, not making ourselves happy. As a result, so many of us approach even our *halaal* sexuality in this way.

So, when we continuously sacrifice ourselves on this altar of unhealthy—and unblessed—servitude until we have nothing left for ourselves, it is only a matter of time before our emotional, mental, and spiritual health suffers, and in a noticeable way. It is for this reason that I think, as part of our healing journey, it is absolutely necessary that we ask our wounded souls and hurting hearts, especially if we have not yet drawn healthy boundaries for ourselves: *What are you investing in, exactly? And why?*

"Boundaries emerge from deep within. They are connected to letting go of guilt and shame, and to changing our beliefs about what we deserve. As our thinking about this becomes clearer, so will our boundaries."

—Melody Beattie, *The Language of Letting Go*

Personal Reflection:
Do you feel that the needs and desires of others, especially in marriage and family relationships, come before your own? Why or why not?

13

Investing in Lasting Love

Earlier, when I was reflecting on my exhaustive self-sacrifice in marriage, I asked my naive, giving soul this question: "What are you investing in, exactly?" And today, if I were to honestly listen to my heart's answer, I think I would hear a younger, naïve version of myself saying, "I'm investing in lasting love."

Looking back, I can see that by not asking for much or by not demanding anything upon entering each marriage (and "almost marriage") that I agreed to, I'd genuinely imagined that I was making a sacrifice today for "happily ever after" tomorrow. In this way, I thought I was investing in lasting love.

I naively imagined that my sacrifices would be counted as proof of my love and commitment to my husband. I thought that by "making things easy" for him—which often included forgoing or delaying some of my basic rights—this would inspire my husband to feel lasting love and commitment toward me. I thought that he in turn would feel inspired to make things easy for me and that he and I would work together nourishing each other's deepest emotional and intimate needs. I thought that through my sacrifices, we would be laying the foundation for "true love."

This vision of lasting love is what I thought I was investing in.

But my experiences have taught me that more often than not, your sacrifices, especially those made at the very beginning of the relationship, will be viewed as your standard of treatment, not as any indication of what you are giving up. Moreover, these sacrifices, no matter how sincere and difficult for you, will not necessarily be viewed as a reflection of the deep love you have for your husband, or the immeasurable value you are bringing to the relationship.

Today, I understand that any sacrifices I make upon entering the relationship are not a guaranteed investment in "something more" later on. Often, they are just a guaranteed investment into a lifetime of "something less."

Naturally, I continue to believe in the beauty and necessity of compassion and sacrifice and making things easier for my soul companion. However, I now believe that this spirit of giving is most meaningful and nourishing for the relationship when it is offered during an unexpected hard time, for example, years into the companionship instead of at the very beginning of it.

At the beginning of any relationship, you are both establishing in the heart of the other person not only who you are, but also the level of care and provision—whether emotional or financial—that you require in a lifelong soul companionship.

Therefore, I believe that for the sake of our long-term emotional, mental, and spiritual health, women should hold men accountable for fulfilling at least the bare minimum of what our All-Wise, Merciful Creator requires of them.

In other words, if a man cannot afford to provide for you on at least the most basic level that you are personally and culturally accustomed to—or if he is unable to offer you the *mahr* that you genuinely desire—then as a general rule (with very rare exceptions, particularly for youth who are just starting out), you shouldn't allow him to marry you until he can.

That patience that you maintain as he "levels up" to what you require, along with that patient perseverance that he maintains as he does the work to earn the title "husband" in your life is what makes for you both investing in lasting love, *bi'idhnillaah*.

"When you refuse to settle for less than the best...the best tends to track you down."
—Mandy Hale, *The Single Woman*

Personal Reflection:

What are your views on how a woman should enter into a relationship? Do you think it's wise for her to forgo some of her basic rights if she feels she has met a really good man? Why or why not?

14

Some Men Are Worth the Sacrifice?

When I speak of requiring men to "level up" to their role as husband before marrying them, I am not suggesting that we intentionally make things difficult for our potential soul companion. I'm suggesting that we as women be honest with ourselves regarding our deepest emotional and spiritual needs, and that we understand that nourishing these needs is directly related to what we voluntarily accept (and require) from a soul companion in marriage.

What our All-Wise, Merciful Creator chooses to test us with that is beyond our control is completely different from what we voluntarily and willingly put on our own souls in the name of love.

When we find ourselves making unnecessary sacrifices so willingly and eagerly after we meet a man whom we imagine we are deeply connected to, it behooves us to take a step back and honestly ask ourselves, Why? If we are honest with ourselves—or are self-aware enough—we will likely find that these eager sacrifices are sometimes due to deep-seated insecurity, to unhealed emotional wounds, or to devaluing ourselves in some way (even if subconsciously).

Yet it feels better to tell ourselves that we're making these sacrifices due to our sincere piety, to early investment in lasting love, or to true sacrifice "for the sake of Allah." However, in reality, when we peel back the layers of our heart, these "pretty picture" explanations are often just fear masquerading as faith. We don't want to lose the man, so we go over and beyond in a desperate attempt to have him for ourselves.

But don't misunderstand. I'm not saying that we should *never* make any sacrifices in order to facilitate marriage to the man we want to spend the rest of our lives with. I'm only saying that when we find ourselves so willing and eager to make these sacrifices before genuinely exploring the option of the man himself "leveling up," it is time to do some honest soul searching.

Perhaps after this honest introspection, you will discover that your decision is in fact rooted in a very judicious, healthy choice for your life and soul. But chances are, you will find that somewhere deep inside, there is the fear of losing this man or opportunity for marriage, so you're acting on this deep-seated fear more than you are acting out of genuine love—for yourself or him.

"But some men are worth the sacrifice," we so often say, convincing ourselves that we are being inspired by the beautiful love story of our mother Khadijah (may Allah be pleased with her) and Prophet Muhammad (peace and blessings be upon him).

But in their love story, Prophet Muhammad had already added immeasurable *tangible* value to Khadijah's most valuable assets before the subject of marriage was ever entertained or broached. Moreover, he added this value during a time when the possibility of marrying Khadijah was not even a thought in his mind.

If you are blessed to meet a man who has proven his blessings in your life in this way while the possibility of marriage was not even on the table—even in his mind— then by all means, make the sacrifices you need to make to be with him.

However, before taking that step, I would advise you to consider this genuine possibility: When we as women are experiencing what we imagine to be tangible worldly blessings from a man we are not married to while he is offering these with no strings attached, we are likely just experiencing a man who wishes to get our attention in a way that he couldn't otherwise.

Granted, this doesn't make his motives wrong or sinful. They might in fact be blessed and sincere. Yet still, it does make his motives completely different from those of Prophet Muhammad (peace and blessings be upon him) prior to his marriage to our Mother Khadijah (may Allah be pleased with her).

Because, truly, there is no comparison between an honorable man who knows the responsibility that Allah has placed on him in marriage—and thus wouldn't dream of asking a woman to give up her rights to be with him—and a man who knows full well that he isn't able to fully take care of you in the way his Lord requires. But still, this man strategically places himself in a position in your life so that you would agree to marry him anyway.

"It's true that material wealth does not define a 'real man,' but rather sincerity, good character, and deep spirituality. But it's also true that a man of sincerity, good character, and deep spirituality would never trivialize the weighty role of material wealth in fulfilling his most basic responsibility as a qawwaam—the very definition of a real man— who provides a comfortable life for his wife."

—from the journal of Umm Zakiyyah

Personal Reflection:
What do you believe are reasonable and healthy sacrifices a woman can make when marrying a man she believes will be good for her? What sacrifices would you caution her against? Why?

15

Male Shame Isn't Manly Humility

During one difficult period of my life when I found myself alone after thinking I'd found my "forever person," I wrote this personal reflection in my journal: *Because good men are so rare these days, "good men" get away with doing a lot of toxic, damaging, and hurtful things.* And till today, as I listen to story after story of the emotional pain that women suffer while seeking soul companionship or committing to soul companionship, I find this sobering observation to be heartbreakingly true (and of course, my All-Knowing Merciful Creator knows best).

Today it appears to have become commonplace for "good men" to deceive women, break marriage contracts they've signed, and even seek a wife—in monogamy *and* polygyny—while having no ability or intention of giving this woman even her basic rights to financial provision. These men often seek out good Muslim women of high status and connect to these women emotionally while knowing full well that she eventually will desire a *halaal* relationship with him. I myself experienced the latter in my second "almost marriage."

Then when the idea of marriage is brought up, only then does he disclose his "humble situation." But by then, she is so emotionally invested that she is willing to give up her rights to be with this man. In this, she imagines that his honesty regarding his humble situation reflects a genuinely honest man with humble character underneath.

But too often what we as women interpret as honesty and humility is merely a form of obligatory male shame. This shame stems from the fact that as a Muslim man, he knows full well what His Creator requires of him as a *qawwaam*, yet he is unable to give this to you. Meanwhile, he is fully willing to offer himself up in this role—and to a woman who quite obviously requires a higher level of basic provision.

So, the only way for a "good man" to go about this is to display a level of what appears to be "manly humility" but is really deeply rooted male shame.

For the woman, it is often only after she is married to him that she realizes that his display of humility was only an obligatory façade, which he needed to get her to agree to marry him. But after marriage, he becomes emotionally distant, cold, and even overbearing in his demands on her. He will often nitpick on her faults and even claim that she is the one getting the better deal out of the relationship, even as he is not fully taking care of her.

And so begins the cycle of emotional suffering for an overly generous-hearted woman who imagined she was getting her own version of a man like Prophet Muhammad (peace and blessings be upon him), while she imagined herself to be a lesser version of our Mother Khadijah (may Allah be pleased with her).

When I'm offering advice to women who are healing from this toxic dynamic in a relationship, I remind them to be compassionate with themselves, as their intentions were good. If they are now divorced, I suggest that they remember this if they ever consider marriage again: As a general rule, it is an absolute must that female souls are "evenly yoked" in marriage if our soul companionship is going to nourish our emotional and spiritual health long-term.

I also remind them that it is only human nature for a man to want to feel like a man in a relationship.

Thus, any man who pursues and then marries a woman who is quite obviously "out of his league" will consciously or unconsciously do whatever he can to prove his manhood, not only to her, but also to his own broken soul steeped in male shame.

In this, it is relevant to note that an impoverished man's active pursuit of a woman of higher status is almost always an indication of deep-seated insecurity and unhealed wounds within him. His pursuit of someone he knows full well he cannot take care of—despite the plethora of women of his own status who are available to him for marriage—is in itself evidence of at least two toxic dynamics which will almost always harm the woman's emotional health long-term:

(1) a complete disregard for his divinely mandated responsibility (and bear in mind that if a man is willing to trivialize his obligations to God, then he is utterly incapable of meaningfully fulfilling his obligations to you).

(2) an unhealthy need for external female validation to make him feel worthy inside (and bear in mind that this need will almost always manifest in his relationships with other women, even if only as perpetual unnecessary emotional interactions with them or as a self-assigned role as their advisor or savior).

These toxic dynamics lead to controlling behavior and rash decisions within the marriage itself—like allowing (or even asking) the woman to carry most or all of the financial responsibility, preventing the woman from pursuing her education or hobbies, limiting or forbidding the woman from having a relationship with her family and friends, or marrying an additional wife (whom he also cannot take care of)—as means of proving his manhood.

Nevertheless, the man himself might genuinely imagine his behavior is rooted in healthy male leadership. However, in the experience of the female soul living with him, his behavior will almost always be toxic and damaging to her emotional and spiritual health.

This is because his unhealed internal state makes it utterly impossible for him to humbly and sincerely consider—and respect—her deepest needs, as this will consistently trigger the sore reminder that he never deserved to be with her in the first place.

"Don't play hard to get. Become hard to get. It's called knowing your worth—and then marrying only a man who adds value to your life and soul."

—from the journal of Umm Zakiyyah

Personal Reflection:
Have you ever caved into pressure to lower your standards because you felt you'd met a "good, sincere Muslim" who appeared to have traits of humility and piety? If so, how are you better honoring your value and desires today?

16

Healing the Female Soul

It was after my divorce from Abdullah that I began to feel isolated from the Muslim community at large. After withstanding the daily criticisms, and sometimes slander, in response to my *halaal* life choices, I withdrew from most human interaction.

Where's my village? This is a question that my hurting soul has often asked as I traversed yet another emotional trial without community support.

Even before I faced the difficult personal trial of divorce, I'd suffered mightily from community shaming and public humiliation due to decisions I'd made for the health of my soul.

As I struggled to hold on to my *emaan* while nourishing a healthy relationship with my hurting female soul, I expressed on more than one occasion my complicated relationship with the increasingly toxic aspects within the wider Muslim community. "I feel like I'm in an abusive relationship that I can't get out of," I'd sometimes say.

You see, there's a reason so many believers, especially women, struggle so visibly after divorce. There's a reason so many of them remove their hijab, stop practicing like they used to, or distance themselves from the Muslim community altogether. Their souls are hurting in ways that our spiritual communities are simply not equipped to healthily acknowledge or address.

In this, there are very few (if any) meaningful spiritual *and* emotional resources and support systems for divorced believers in our faith communities. Resources exist almost exclusively for men and women who are married (and in monogamy).

How then are we to be meaningful supporters to each other if the only people who are welcomed in our communities are those who help us improve our public image and "marriage statistics"?

In the Qur'an, Allah says:

يَـٰٓأَيُّهَا ٱلَّذِينَ ءَامَنُوا۟ ٱتَّقُوا۟ ٱللَّهَ حَقَّ تُقَاتِهِۦ وَلَا تَمُوتُنَّ إِلَّا وَأَنتُم مُّسْلِمُونَ ﴿١٠٢﴾

وَٱعْتَصِمُوا۟ بِحَبْلِ ٱللَّهِ جَمِيعًا وَلَا تَفَرَّقُوا۟ وَٱذْكُرُوا۟ نِعْمَتَ ٱللَّهِ عَلَيْكُمْ

"O you who believe! Fear Allah as He should be feared, and die not except in a state of Islam [as Muslims] with complete submission. And hold fast, all of you together, to the Rope of Allah, and do not become divided amongst yourselves, and remember Allah's Favor on you…"
—*Ali 'Imraan* (3:102-103)

Yet for divorced women, who is there to help us hold on to the Rope of Allah? And who is there who even genuinely cares whether or not we remain part of the Muslim community at large?

For so many of us, deep emotional wounds turn into deep spiritual wounds. So after a difficult life trial like divorce, we find ourselves in an emotional whirlwind of pain while drowning in the dark waters of spiritual confusion, barely holding on to our faith—like I myself did when parting from my first soul companion.

To make matters worse, when we are facing this life-altering trial, we often find ourselves surrounded by loved ones who do not understand (or agree with) our journey. Meanwhile, we are immersed in faith communities that seem to have only the spiritual capacity to speak about divorce as something that Shaytaan loves or as an "epidemic" or "crisis" that needs to be rooted out of our communities like a destructive social disease.

In viewing divorce through this narrow lens, our spiritual leaders, as well as our sisters and brothers in faith, thereby imply—and often state outright—that anyone who chooses divorce is an agent of Shaytaan or a victim of his plotting. In this—whether due to sincere ignorance or the willful desire to shame and humiliate divorced believers under the misguided assumption that this will somehow magically "cure the divorce disease"—our faith communities ignore the fact that soul destruction is so much more dangerous (and exponentially more beloved to Shaytaan) than someone's divorce status.

Nevertheless, it is indeed true that Shaytaan and his agents rejoice in inciting divorce between a man and a woman who are beneficial soul companions for each other. However, it is also true that Shaytaan and his agents rejoice *more* in inciting anything that would cause a believer to destroy their soul.

Thus, if Shaytaan and his agents are able to incite two believers who are obviously toxic for each other to stay together in the name of "till death do us part" while one or both of them lose their soul, then this is much more beloved to the devil and his agents than any divorce.

For this reason, we need to understand that when a sincere believer chooses divorce, they are often merely choosing their emotional and spiritual health over the loss of their soul. Therefore, we should offer them compassion and support on their healing journey, instead of becoming agents of Shaytaan ourselves as we shame and humiliate them until they feel unwelcomed even in the ummah of Islam.

"The parable of the believers in their affection, mercy, and compassion for each other is that of a body. When any limb aches, the whole body reacts with sleeplessness and fever."

—Prophet Muhammad (peace and blessings be upon him)
Sahih Bukhari 5665, Sahih Muslim 2586

Personal Reflection:
Have you ever abandoned a believer emotionally or spiritually due to a *halaal* personal decision they made in marriage or divorce? How are you showing more empathy and compassion to others today?

17

Beautiful Storms of Life

The other day I lay awake with a heavy heart, so I asked myself, "If you could think of one thing you've been given in this world that you are most grateful for because it has brought your life the most joy, tranquility and blessings, what would it be?"

Moments later tears welled in my eyes and I broke down crying—because right then, Allah placed in my heart the unwavering realization that the very trial that was distressing me most had brought the most joy, tranquility, and blessings into my life—both worldly and spiritual.

SubhaanAllaah...

So often when we are recovering from a difficult trial, we focus on what we lost. In this, we are like survivors of a severe storm returning to our home to survey the damage, and we become devastated by what's before us. We see our precious belongings destroyed, charred, or buried in debris, and we wonder how we'll survive without the things we'd come to depend on for so long. In that moment, things we invested so much of our time and wealth into are gone, and we have no idea where to go from there.

Such are the storms of life, and no soul can avoid them.

Just as no season in nature is without its storms, no life in this world is without its storms.

So dear soul, remember this:

Even when so much falls apart and failure seems inevitable, everything is coming together in the perfect imperfection that defines the highest potential for any human soul. The "falling bricks" of life are merely forming your pathway to reach whatever is meant for you—and to guard you from whatever is not meant to be. Even in the magnificence of nature, our Creator shows us that beauty is not manifested in only straight lines and "perfect" outcomes. Storms and loss sweep through the landscapes of nature just as they will sweep through the landscapes of your soul.

"Amazing is the affair of the believer. Verily, every affair of his is good, and this is for no one except the believer. If something of good [or happiness] befalls him, he is grateful, and that is good for him. If something of harm befalls him, he is patient, and that is good for him."

—Prophet Muhammad (peace and blessings be upon him)
Sahih Muslim #2999

Personal Reflection:

Think of a painful trial you faced in the past. How are you benefiting emotionally, spiritually, and personally from this trial today?

Epilogue

A Letter to My Beautiful, Imperfect Soul

Four years ago, I wrote a letter (as italicized below) to the hurting little girl inside me, and today I am humbled and grateful that I am, by the mercy and permission of Allah, fulfilling the promise that I made to her that day.

At the time, she and I were at the beginning of our beautiful, imperfect journey that we continue to take together today. This is a journey that allows me to enjoy a life of soul-nourishing gratitude and solitude that is much better than the best I could have hoped for or imagined when we first began.

Dear gentle soul,

I will never disrespect you ever again, bi'idhnillaah. I will never again lower my standards and forsake my rights in seeking to make a man's life easier.

From this day forward, dear gentle soul, I choose you. You've suffered so much in this world, and I'm deeply sorry to inflict this pain on you, too.

But don't fret, dear soul, I now know better so I'm now going to do better. And I beseech my Merciful Rabb for help in my heart making hijrah from this toxic relationship that has crushed and discarded you.

You will stand tall again, bi'idhnillaah, and you will smile again. Even if another man never again shares your bed or journey in this world.

Choose the libaas of taqwaa, dear soul, and Allah will forever honor and protect you.

With love and gratitude,

Umm Zakiyyah
August 30, 2024
26th of Safar 1446AH

Closing Notes

From the Journal of Umm Zakiyyah

Dear struggling soul,

All you can do is the best you can.

No, your best won't be *the* best, but that's okay. It's the best you can do. And your Merciful Rabb (Lord and Creator) knows this and still accepts your efforts from you.

A prophetic teaching that reminds us of this can be found in the words of a du'aa (prayerful supplication) we are instructed to say every morning and evening:

"O Allah, You are my Rabb, none has the right to be worshipped except You. You created me and I am Your servant, and I abide to Your covenant and promise as best I can. I take refuge in You from the evil of which I have committed. I acknowledge Your favor upon me, and I acknowledge my sin; so forgive me, for verily none can forgive sin except You" (Bukhari).

SubhaanAllah…

At the very moment we are asking for forgiveness for falling short in fulfilling our duty to Allah, we are instructed to say, "I abide to Your covenant and promise as best I can." In these prophetic words, we are reminded that our absolute best will always be imperfect, and that's okay.

So please stop stressing over your faults and sins, even as you continue to strive against them and feel healthy regret. Just continue to show gratefulness to Allah and believe in Him, while trusting that He will not punish you for being an imperfect human. Even on your best days, there's nothing else you can be.

In the Qur'an our Merciful Creator says:

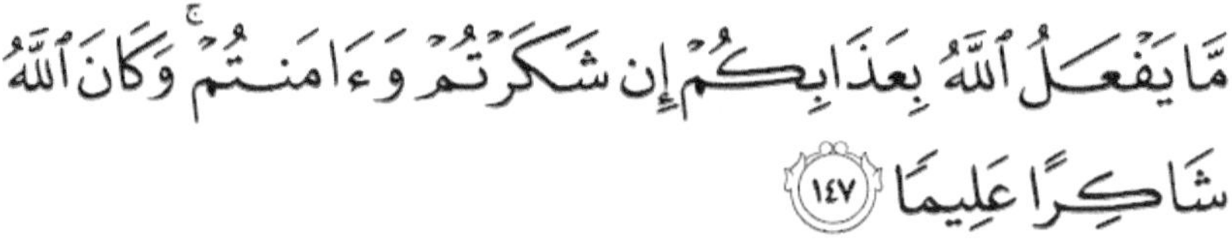

"Why should Allah punish you if you have thanked (Him) and have believed in Him. And Allah is Ever All-Appreciative (of good), All-Knowing."
—*An-Nisaa'* (4:147)

Before You Become His Garment in Marriage: Do's and Don'ts for Muslim Women

by Umm Zakiyyah

I remember when I first began getting official marriage proposals. I was around seventeen years old. I had a long list of questions I would ask anyone who came to ask about me.

Years later my daughter's father would tell me he felt like he was taking a test and solving "brain teaser" puzzles. He'd say it jokingly, and we'd both get a good laugh out of it.

At the time, I had written down as many questions as I could think of, and for me at the time, that represented my level best of showing up authentically as myself.

Once I selected my soul companion for marriage, I was mentally prepared to do everything I could to serve and please him and avoid even the chance of divorce. As a youth, I genuinely imagined that this was everything I needed to go into a marriage fully prepared and to protect my marriage from ever dying.

However, over the years, life has taught me that, as undesirable as divorce is, there are things worse than a dying marriage—the worst of which is a dying soul. I learned that you could stay married and lose yourself. I learned that you could never even consider divorce but lose your faith. I learned that you could look happy on the outside and be suffering emotional pain on the inside. I learned that you could preserve your relationships with your husband and loved ones while sacrificing your relationship with Allah.

When I booked my official first RTT session as a client, I wanted to find out why I so often woke up feeling emotionally exhausted, mentally spent, and overcome with weighty dread about facing the day ahead. I also wanted to understand why it was so challenging for me to show up for myself with joy, mental calm, and self-love.

I had already done a psychotherapy session with another therapy practitioner and had been part of numerous support groups over the years. But still, I kept hitting these roadblocks: I struggled to actually enjoy my daily self-care routines, I found it difficult to feel comfortable and at ease while expanding my business, and

I continuously felt disinclined to move forward with so many of the things I loved and wanted in my life.

During the RTT session, my therapist asked me to take in a deep breath and relax (as is standard in a Rapid Transformational Therapy session) so that I could quiet the chatter of my conscious mind and calmly recall what was at the root of these roadblocks. In this, she was guiding me to relax my overall nervous system and thus activate a parasympathetic response. This relaxation technique allowed me to access the pictures and words stored in the "safety toolbox" of my mind that discouraged me from showing up to my life with joy, mental calm, and self-love.

In one scene (which is what we call a mental memory in RTT) I saw myself at around fourteen years old sitting in the passenger seat of a car next to a male relative (whom I'll call Walad) who was about ten years my elder and had come to the city to visit our family.

In this scene, I saw Walad become suddenly angry with me then threaten to forcibly remove me from his car and abandon me on the side of the road. In the mental memory, I recalled learning that this threat of violence had erupted due to me expressing a different perspective from him during a casual conversation we'd been having as he drove me home.

After this scene replayed in my mind, I was asked to link this incident (and two other earlier mental memories) to my current mental roadblocks. In other words, my therapist was asking me to connect this memory of Walad to the reason that it was so difficult for me to embrace joy, mental peace, and self-love and to pursue the life I wanted while fully embracing the things I loved.

As my RTT practitioner and I discussed the links between these early mental memories and how I showed up in my life today, I was surprised that there had been any significant link at all between Walad's treatment of me when I was a teenager and how I showed up for myself as a grown woman.

Consciously, after repeated negative and threatening experiences with Walad, I had told myself years ago that I would simply keep ties with him and treat him kindly, but otherwise I'd keep my distance since he was so mercurial, unsafe, and potentially violent.

As my therapist and I continued exploring what had actually come up while my nervous system was in a relaxed state, I realized that this "moving picture" in my mind from fourteen years old (along with a couple of others) had implanted the following "feeling words" in my nafs and were then mentally stored in the "safety toolbox" of my mind:

As a female soul in this world, it's not safe for you to feel relaxed and carefree because this could expose you to danger or abandonment. As a female, your job is to shrink yourself to make sure that the men in your life feel good about themselves and are not offended or angered by your thoughts and feelings. So, as a woman, it's not safe for you to pursue the things you want and love. Besides, as a "good Muslim woman," you'll one day have to give up everything that makes you happy if the man in your life wants you to, even if you're doing nothing wrong or displeasing to your Creator.

That's when I had another epiphany. Nearly every single man I had allowed into my intimate space emotionally (whether in considering marriage or entering marriage itself) held some version of one or more of these beliefs about women in relation to himself:

You don't have the right to think, feel, or express anything I don't like. It is your job to patiently stand by my side while I freely live my life and do whatever I want, even if it hurts you deeply. If you're really a good woman, you would give up everything you want to make me happy. It is your job to keep quiet and learn from me because none of your knowledge or experience matters if it doesn't align with mine. I value your intelligence and talents only insomuch as they make me feel good about myself for "conquering" or "owning" someone like you.

Then I recalled that I had experienced over and over some version of the initial Walad incident in so many of my interactions with men later in life. Realizing this inspired a deeper epiphany for me: The picture that I had in my mind of what a "man" looked like was various versions of Walad: threatening, entitled, and insecure.

So, unconsciously, I'd felt that the most that I could hope for in a good man was that he wasn't threatening. Anything else (i.e. entitlement and insecurity), I'd unconsciously assumed, came along with having any man at all.

That was why when I looked for a "good man," I'd continuously sought or accepted someone who "wouldn't mind" if I pursued the things I loved and wanted in life. What this meant in practical reality was securing for myself a "man in flesh" who was a manifestation of the unconscious plea of the shrinking little girl inside me: *I know it disturbs you deeply that I have a life outside of you, but please just don't harm me emotionally, verbally, or physically whenever I do the things I love. That's all I ask.*

It was both chilling and profound to discover that I had been living all my adult life—even as a forty something divorced woman now on my own—shrinking and apologizing to men for my existence as an intelligent, vibrant female soul in this world. That was when I realized it was time for me to reembrace my worth and honor my needs…

READ MORE

at
uzauthor.com *or* **uzhearthub.com**

Before YOU BECOME HIS GARMENT in Marriage
Do's & Don'ts for Muslim Women!
UMM ZAKIYYAH

Glossary of Arabic and Islamic Terms

Allah: Arabic term for God; the only One who has the right to be worshipped

'aqeedah: foundational beliefs of the Islamic spiritual way of life

ayah: verse from Qur'an or divine sign

bi'idhnillaah: "with the help of Allah (the Creator)"

du'aa: prayerful supplication; informal prayer

emaan: sincere faith; authentic spirituality; belief in Islam

fitnah: difficult trial

halaal: divinely blessed or permissible

haraam: divinely forbidden or sinful

hijrah: migration from one land to another for the sake of your faith

khayr: blessed goodness or divine blessing

khula': female-initiation marriage dissolution

libaas: garment or clothing

mahr: obligatory gift given to woman upon marriage; dowry

nafs: inner-self or desires that are self-serving and spiritually harmful

nikaah: Islamic marriage contract; often written and signed before the man and woman live together

qawwaam: the man's divinely assigned role of being the maintainer, provider, and protector of women in the home and society

Rabb: another name for Allah that refers to His Lordship over creation; Creator, Owner and Manager of all that exists

sadaqah: voluntary, non-obligatory charity

sallallaahu'alaihi wa sallam: prayers of peace and blessing (upon the Prophet)

Shaytaan: the devil; Satan

SubhaanAllah: statement of glorification of Allah: "Glory to Allah, and Exalted and High is He above any imperfection"

Sunnah: prophetic guidance or example; the life and teachings of Prophet Muhammad (peace and blessings be upon him)

tafseer: authentic interpretation and spiritual explanation of the
 Qur'an
tajweed: rules of reciting the Qur'an
taqwaa: sincere God-consciousness and daily soul care that
 protects the heart from corruption and the soul from
 spiritual harm in the Hereafter
ummah: worldwide faith community

About the Author

Known for her soul-touching books and spiritual reflections on emotional healing, Umm Zakiyyah is a world-renowned author, speaker, and soul-care mentor. She specializes in supporting women of faith transform into the best version of themselves—personally, emotionally, and spiritually.

Also known by her birth name Ruby Moore and her "Muslim name" Baiyinah Siddeeq, Umm Zakiyyah is the internationally acclaimed, award-winning author of more than forty books, including novels, short stories, and self-help. Her books are used in high schools and universities in the United States and worldwide, and her work has been translated into multiple languages.

Her novel *His Other Wife* is now a short film (available on Prime Video).

Umm Zakiyyah is certified in Rapid Transformational Therapy ® (RTT) and hypnotherapy, qualifications she earned under the guidance of Marisa Peer, author of *I Am Enough*.

Umm Zakiyyah is a certified member of IACT (International Association of Counselors and Therapists) and an executive member of IICT (International Institute of Complementary Therapists).

Umm Zakiyyah studied Arabic, Qur'an, Islamic sciences, *'aqeedah,* and *tafseer* in the USA, Egypt, and Saudi Arabia for more than fifteen years.

Umm Zakiyyah has a BA degree in Elementary Education, an MA in English Language Learning, and

Cambridge's CELTA (Certificate in English Language Teaching to Adults).

She is currently based in Dallas, Texas (USA).

Connect with her online:
UZ books: uzauthor.com
Therapy, coaching, and mentorship: sqsoul.com
UZ courses: uzhearthub.com and uzuniversity.com
Instagram: @uzauthor

Read FREE Books by Umm Zakiyyah